MW01291487

40 KEYS
TO BEING A
FAVORED
FATHER

Dr. Jerry A. Grillo, Jr.

40 KEYS TO BEING A FAVORED FATHER

Copyright 2006
FZM Publishing
P.O. Box 3707 Hickory, N.C. 28603

IBSN 978-1-4960-6387-8

Second Print 2008
Third Print 2014

TABLE OF CONTENT

INTRODUCTION

CONCLUSION

DECISION PAGE

INTRODUCTION

Fathers are the bedrock of society. When families fall apart, society falls into social and cultural decline. Ultimately, the breakdown of the American family is at the root of nearly every other social problem and pathology.

Not long ago, most children in America grew up in solid, two-parent families. Today children who do so are a minority. Illegitimacy, divorce and other lifestyle choices have radically altered the American family, thereby altering the social landscape. The person who sticks around to bear the burden and joy of raising the family is the mother. If we continue on this decline, we're going to see more grandparents raising their grandchildren now that this curse is seeping into both parents. We need to awaken the spirit of the father. Fathers, it's time to stand and fight! It's time for us to raise the flag; to declare that we've had enough of this satanic attack on our species.

This book is not an exhaustive study on parenting nor is it supposed to be a manual for raising children. I have placed 40 keys that I believe will help you get on the right track to being a favored father.

Take each key daily and mediate on it. Let them sink in to your spirit and I promise that you will see change, not only in your life, but also in those around you.

I have labored to condense each thought to a specific point. Go slow; take it in with much thought. If you are a father, use them; if not, learn from them. You may become one in the future.

What Makes A Dad

God took the strength of a mountain, The majesty of a
tree,
The warmth of a summer sun, The calm of a quiet sea,
The generous soul of nature, The comforting arm of
night,
The wisdom of the ages, The power of the eagle's flight,
The joy of a morning in spring, The faith of a mustard
seed,
The patience of eternity, The depth of a family need.

Then God combined these qualities, When there was
nothing more to add.
He knew His masterpiece was complete,
And so, He called it ... Dad

Author unknown

ALLOW ACCESS

Our example of being a good father should come from the greatest father that exists, God!
*"...God through our Lord Jesus Christ, through whom we have **gained access** by faith into this grace in which we now stand..."*
Romans 5:1-2 NIV

As good fathers, we need to give more access to our children. For men to allow access, they first have to learn how to approach God and His throne for themselves. Men have a hard time allowing others in their atmospheres who do not challenge them to conquer or to fight for increase. This is why men find it so difficult to just let our children or spouse in our world. We try to keep them at a distance and our children know and feel that limited access.

"For through him we both have access to the Father by one Spirit." Ephesians 2:18 NIV

God sent Jesus so that we would have access to him. God, as our Father, was letting us know that He has an open door policy to Him. As fathers, we should reciprocate the same feelings to those that are called sons (no gender).

Access means the right to enter, or approach; the act of coming toward or nearer without being in trouble. Good fathers have an atmosphere that provides their children with access to them any time of day. Our legacy is not in what we do. Our children are our legacy!

2

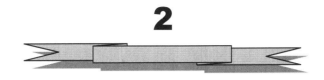

AVAILABILITY IS PROOF THAT YOU CARE

"ACCESS IS PROVEN BY BEING AVAILABLE."

THE GREATEST GIFT I EVER HAD CAME FROM GOD, AND I CALL HIM DAD!

You may be thinking that being available is the same thing as being accessible. **I assure you it is not!** We have learned responses to those around us. Why is it that we tend to give more time to those who have no real connection to us and less time to those who really are connected to our future...**our children**?

What makes us a favored father in the eyes of God is when we can make the time and energy necessary to give our offspring great availability. Men have a terrible time recognizing and understanding that any time we spend with our children, even time we think is mundane, is still valuable and great time in their eyes.

What if God treated us the same? What if every time we approached God we felt as if we were bothering him... that we were the last thing He wanted in His atmosphere? I tell you today, what our youth need more than video games...

television... clothes... food... friends... education... is to experience the joy of having an available father.

.

- *Available fathers produce comfort.*
- *Available fathers produce peace.*
- *Available fathers provide security.*

Let your children feel they have you...be available!

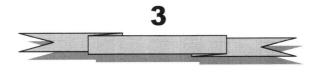

DEAL WITH YOUR ANGER

IF THE NEW AMERICAN FATHER FEELS BEWILDERED AND
EVEN DEFEATED, LET HIM TAKE COMFORT FROM THE FACT
THAT WHAT-EVER HE DOES IN ANY FATHERING SITUATION
HAS A FIFTY PERCENT CHANCE OF BEING RIGHT.
BILL COSBY

When it comes to this world, we have all failed
tremendously as fathers. This is the reason for this quote.
There really are no books that entirely speak to us as
fathers in helping us to raise our children, except the Word
of God. This is usually the most overlooked book in our
libraries.

*"In your anger do not sin; when you are on your beds,
search your hearts and be silent." Psalms 4:4 NIV*

*" In your anger do not sin: Do not let the sun go down
while you are still angry, and do not give the devil a
foothold." Ephesians 4:26-27 NIV*

God never said that we wouldn't get angry or mad. He just
said to deal with it. He said for us to control it and not
allow it to control us. We have too often, in our anger,
sliced wounds in the hearts of the innocent that will take a

lifetime to heal. Favored fathers grab hold of their anger swiftly so that their words will not destroy but instruct.

We are most definitely going to be angered by those around us. Let's make up our minds today that we are going to control our reactions and stop hurting those around us.

4

SHOW AFFECTION

IT IS MUCH EASIER TO **BECOME** A FATHER THAN **TO BE ONE**.
AUTHOR: KENT NERBURN

*"The LORD did not set his affection on you and choose you
because you were more numerous than other peoples, for
you were the fewest of all peoples. But it was because the
LORD loved you…"Deuteronomy 7:7-8 NIV*

Here is a hard one for most men to swallow; learning to be
affectionate and showing it to those they love. The
dictionary defines the word **affection as a mental or
emotional state or tendency; disposition or feeling fond
or tender feeling; warm liking.**

You may be saying, ***"I do love my children."*** Let me be
clear; affection doesn't mean to love someone. It means to
show love and to express it in word and deed. I know the
old saying, *"if I put a roof over their heads and clothing on
their backs, that says that I love them."* **Come on**! You
know children need more than things. Yes, providing for
them is honorable and noble but to be a favored father you
are going to have to go deeper. You are going to have to
express your love in words, hugs and gifts.

Wrap your arms around your son and watch him melt. Give

your daughter a kiss on the cheek and let her realize no man will ever love her as much as her father will. This will cause the power of God's favor to explode in your life. You are on your way to being a favored father.

WALK IN COMMITMENT

"ONE FATHER IS MORE THAN A HUNDRED SCHOOLMASTERS."
GEORGE HERBERT

A favored father must show and exemplify what it means to have commitment. Sons must witness that there are some things that are worth standing for. One of the greatest crises in this country is that no one wants to take a stand! No one wants to have enemies.

Taking a stand, or better, picking a side will always create an enemy.

Commitment means a pledge or promise to do something; a dedication to a long-term course of action, engagement or action.

Commitment is being steady in your life to live out the message of righteousness rather than always preaching about it. I once heard a father say to his children that the reason he didn't go to church was because it was his job as a father to point the way to church. That's crazy! Let's stop pointing and start leading the way as favored fathers.

- *Commitment teaches stamina in hard times.*

- *Commitment produces character.*
- *Commitment provides stability.*
- *Commitment is a decision and not a feeling.*

6

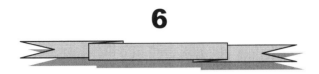

PROVIDE COMFORT

"Comfort, comfort my people, says your God. Speak tenderly to Jerusalem, and proclaim to her that her hard service has been completed, that her sin has been paid for…" Isaiah 40:1-2 NIV

"IT MAY SERVE AS A COMFORT TO US, IN ALL OUR CALAMITIES AND AFFLICTIONS, THAT HE THAT LOSES ANYTHING AND GETS WISDOM BY IT IS A GAINER BY THE LOSS." L. ESTRANGE

A father's job is to create a climate of comfort, to soothe in times of distress and to lift the hopes in times of defeat. No matter what, life is going to treat our children the same way it has treated us. There will always be times of hardship and pain. A favored father is a father who takes the time to comfort his family.

Maybe we should turn off the television at times, go and sit on the edge of our children's bed and allow them to experience the presence of their father while they are drifting off to sleep. There is no better calm to a child than to feel the warmth of their father in the room.

- ***Comfort produces confidence.***
- ***Comfort allows freedom to exist in the house.***
- ***Comfort produces hope.***
- ***Comfort makes the hard place easy to live in***.

Be a father who creates a climate of comfort and peace to your atmosphere.

7

BUILD CONFIDENCE

"For the LORD will be your confidence and will keep your foot from being snared." Proverbs 3:26 NIV

CONFIDENCE IS A FIRM BELIEF SYSTEM... A FIRM RELIANCE... A FIRM TRUST IN ONE'S ABILITY TO ACHIEVE AND SUCCEED IN WHATEVER HE OR SHE SETS OUT TO ACCOMPLISH.

Often there are psychological dysfunctions in homes that are void of a father. A child's confidence is fed by the father and nurtured by the mother.

A favored father must walk and teach confidence. You can't succeed without confidence. It takes confidence in God to believe on His Word. It takes confidence to move toward areas of uncertainty. Children who are fearful usually haven't experienced a supportive and confident father.

My children are allowed to try any sport or take on any endeavor, as long as it doesn't compromise their faith. I can tell you that if I push them and speak words of victory and success to them, you can see and feel it in their atmosphere.

Fathers are the confidence builder in their home.

- *Confidence causes the weak to face their fears.*
- *Confidence creates boldness.*
- *Confidence builds trust in ones actions.*
- *Confidence decides movement.*

8

GIVE COMPLIMENTS

Compliment often!

Look at the definition of the word compliment: ***"That which brings to completion or perfection, something added to complete the whole."*** I like that!

Men have a hard time being verbal with compliments. We often ignore what has been done around us. We tend to take for granted what our spouse has done every day to bring comfort to our lives. Real men who understand motivation will learn how to complement those around them. Don't be a person who only speaks up when something isn't right. Take the time to let others know what is right and not what's wrong.

When a father compliments his spouse, he creates a memory in his children that she matters and what she does is important to him. His focus on her achievements in the house proves that little things matter. We must stop absentee fathers. Our families need to hear the voice of the father complimenting them and inspiring them to greatness.

- ***Complimenting creates joy rather than irritation in a task.***

- *Complimenting makes mistakes much easier to take.*
- *Complimenting those around you pushes them to succeed.*

LEARN TO COMMUNICATE

Communication is the one thing that really separates us from the animal kingdom. The ability to be able to communicate is the source of unity.

Talking does not necessarily mean you are communicating. To communicate, the other party must understand what you are trying to expose or to reveal. Communication is to pass along information in part, or in whole, by ways of expressions and words. When a child is born, they are born as an empty canvas. They have no ideologies. They possess no fears. They have no racial preference…a blank canvas; that's all they are. The communicative father learns to dip his brush of love, hope and peace into the colors of words and deeds. In doing so, he is painting on the souls of his children what they will actually become.

Take the time to learn how to communicate effectively. Your children are worth the time. Be a Michael Angelo and paint your masterpiece, not on a church ceiling or on a glass window, but on the heart of your family.

Dip your brush in the Holy Spirit and paint away. Communicate to your family that you love them…that you need them…that you can't live without them.

- *Communication stops arguments.*
- *Communication provides understanding.*
- *Communication requires wisdom.*

ACTIVATE COURAGE

"Be strong and courageous, because you will lead these people to inherit the land I swore to their forefathers to give them. Be strong and very courageous." Joshua 1:6-7 NIV

To be a favored father and do what is right in the eyes of God, it will require incredible courage. With all the negative publicity about raising our families with Godly principles, it's no wonder the church is decreasing instead of increasing in power. Too many fathers are compromising so they can feel that they fit in. Avoid this way of thinking. It's better to be the outcast in society than to be an outcast in heaven.

It takes a brave man to stand up for what he believes in and to not be ashamed to teach his children the right way. When you see a successful business or family, it's because someone made a courageous decision.

"...choose for yourselves this day whom you will serve... But as for me and my household, we will serve the LORD." Joshua 24:15 NIV

- *Courage produces success.*
- *Courage builds confidence in your followers.*

- *Courage helps others stand tall.*
- *Courage keeps faith alive.*
- *It takes courage to serve God.*

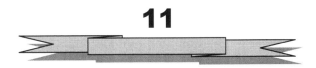

DEMONSTRATE DEVOTION

"Stablish (establish) thy word unto thy servant, who is devoted to thy fear." Psalms 119:38

Devoted means to be dedicated, to be consecrated, to be loving, to be loyal, and faithful. We need some devoted fathers in our churches.

Let me give you an acronym on the word- D.A.D.D.Y.

I wrote a book when I was a youth pastor called, "DADDY GOD." The purpose of the book was to describe what a good and great God we serve.

Are you?
- **Dedicated...** Loyal to your spouse, loyal to your children? Dedicated fathers walk in faithfulness.
- **Affectionate...** Learn to hug, and express your feelings and emotions.
- **Determined...** To do what's right will require determination.
- **Denied...** Let your family know they will not be denied your love.
- **You** are always on His mind. Our children need to know that they are always on your mind.

Be a devoted Father. Be a father that teaches and lives a devoted lifestyle. God will place the same focus on you as you place on your family. Be more devoted to them than you are your career, hobbies and friends.

12

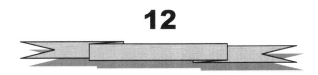

BE CONSIDERATE
(DON'T BE SWIFT TO SAY "NO")

"For all the promises of God in Him are Yes, and in Him Amen, to the glory of God through us." 2 Corinthians 1:20-21 NKJV

I don't know about you but one of my worst habits used to be immediately saying "no" to what my children would ask me. I had the hardest time in this area until one afternoon. My son came to me to ask once again if one of his friends could spend the night at our house. I was immediately irritated and said **"NO."** He look at me with those disappointed eyes and said, "You always say **NO!**"

When he left my presence I said to myself, "**that is not true**; I don't always say no." The Spirit of the Lord responded to me and in my heart I heard him say, *"YES, YOU DO!"*

The Holy Spirit dealt with me on the reason why I always say no. He showed me that I was concerned about my son and his wishes, but that I didn't want **my** world to be interrupted. The question that came to me from the Lord hurt deep… **WHY DID YOU HAVE CHILDREN IF YOU WEREN'T GOING TO LET LIFE BE INTERRUPTED?**

Since then, there are kids at my house often. I seem to have become a dad to a few boys that have no dad at home. Life is good. I love my children more since I am willing to allow them to interrupt my life.

13

BE AN ENCOURAGER

OUTSTANDING FATHERS GO OUT OF THEIR WAY TO BOOST THE SELF-ESTEEM OF THEIR CHILDREN. IF YOUR CHILDREN BELIEVE IN THEMSELVES, IT'S AMAZING WHAT THEY CAN ACCOMPLISH.

"Therefore encourage one another and build each other up...warn those who are idle, encourage the timid, help the weak, be patient with everyone." 1 Thessalonians 5:11, 14 NIV

Encouraging your children to get up after they have fallen is better than correcting them in their mistakes. Think for a moment how we enjoy being encouraged by those above us more than being corrected. That's not to say that there is not a proper place for discipline. However, it is obvious that the youth around us are missing being encouraged in the proper and right things of life.

To encourage means to build courage, hope and confidence. It means to give support. The world is encouraging our children to live contrary to the things of God. They encourage them to find their own way and to make adult decisions with a child like mentality. If we fathers don't stand in the gap and become encouragers… motivators… coaches to your families, someone else will.

Satan hasn't left them alone. Why have we?

- *An encourager creates pleasant memories.*
- *An encourager builds the heart of failure to try again.*
- *An encourager is more like our heavenly Father.*
- *An encourager forces the will to want to change.*

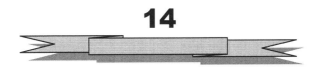

14

Equip and Train

*"May the God of peace… **equip** you with everything good for doing his will, and may he work in us what is pleasing to him, through Jesus Christ, to whom be glory for ever and ever. Amen." Hebrews 13:20-21 NIV*

Equip means to supply special tools. Equipment is something that is needed to fulfill ones purpose. The job of a favored father is to provide the necessary environment for their family to succeed. This is not to say that they have to have what their friends have. You may not financially be in a position to buy what others have, but to be a favored father you must do your best.

I have witnessed in my lifetime fathers who would spend more on their hobbies and habits than they would on taking care of the needs of their children.

HINTS TO EQUIP:
- *Equip them to understand their faith in Jesus Christ.*
- *Equip them with an education.*
- *Equip them with confidence by encouraging them to try.*
- *Equip them with peace of mind by sharing your life openly.*

- ***Equip them with everything they will need to win.***

God has taken the necessary steps to assure us that we are equipped to win. Let us do the same with our family.

15

CELEBRATE THEIR SUCCESS

A favored father shows excitement about his children's success and accomplishments.

So often our children are a part of activities that seem meaningless to us, but our ability to express excitement over their interests will build a mentality to strive for success in our children.

Children need affirmation in their performance, good or bad. Often fathers ignore the success of their children. This will birth feelings of insignificance in their minds.

Sometimes it may be boring and time consuming to sit and watch a play or a game when you could be doing something more creative. Trust me; they are looking at the sidelines to see if you are watching their accomplishments. When you give a thumbs up or a big smile, you shoot straight into their hearts and place a memory in their minds of what a real father is all about.

Your child will have a much better understanding of what God is all about. You are actually showing them what a good Father God they have when you exemplify a favored father.

16

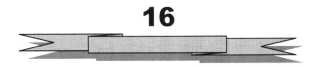

UNMASK YOUR EMOTIONS

"My tears have been my food day and night." Psalms 42:3
NIV

WHEN DEALING WITH PEOPLE, REMEMBER YOU ARE NOT
DEALING WITH CREATURES OF LOGIC, BUT CREATURES OF
EMOTION. ~DALE CARNEGIE

LET'S NOT FORGET THAT THE LITTLE EMOTIONS ARE THE
GREAT CAPTAINS OF OUR LIVES AND WE OBEY THEM
WITHOUT REALIZING IT. ~VINCENT VAN GOGH, 1889

For years, men have been conditioned to think that to show
their feelings is a sign of weakness. This is not true. **Real
men cry**! **Real men worship**! Real men have feelings and
are not ashamed to show them to others. Our children need
to see our feelings, especially our sons.

I can remember the first time I witnessed my dad crying.
Mind you, I witnessed my father fall from a two-story
house and not shed one tear. He's from the old school that
real men don't cry. It was a Sunday night and I was at the
altar giving my heart to the Lord when I heard this crying
taking place behind me. I turned my head to see who it was
and to my astonishment, it was my dad. He was crying and

to watch those tears leave his eyes in the presence of God, gave me a memory that I will never forget. My dad is human!

- *Emotional release is healthy for the mind.*
- *Emotional worship enters the heart of God.*

17

DISCIPLINE

"My son, do not despise the LORD's discipline and do not resent his rebuke, because the LORD disciplines those he loves, as a father the son he delights in." Proverbs 3:11-12 NIV

"Train a child in the way he should go, and when he is old he will not turn from it." Proverbs 22:6 NIV

To train someone you will have to first be willing to discipline him or her. To discipline does not necessarily mean that you have to hit them or punish them. It does mean that you must take the time to instruct them.

Disciplining is not easy. It takes time to train someone. Favored fathers will take the time necessary to train, instruct and teach their children how to win in all things. I love spending time with my son. I enjoy sitting around watching television or going to a movie with him. It is in those times that I find the best time to train him. *Discipline is training that develops self-control, character; discipline creates order and efficiency in others.*

- ***Discipline produces disciples.***
- ***Discipline demoralizes slothfulness.***
- ***Discipline creates focus.***

- ***Discipline proves love.***
- ***Discipline builds security.***

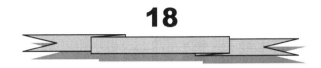

18

CONTROL YOUR FRUSTRATIONS

I promise you, this one is hard! I can't count on my hand the times I have leaked my frustrations on my family, my church and those around me.

If you live a normal life, you are going to experience frustration. A favored father learns how to funnel his frustration into energy and not anger. I was watching a scene in a store one day. A parent was shopping and becoming frustrated with the crowd at the store. The little girl was walking beside them, holding their hand, when she saw something on the shelf that attracted her. She stopped for a brief moment to see. What happened next made my blood boil. The parent looked at this child with a face that could have killed an army and pulled with such force that I really thought they would have pulled that little arm right out the socket. I wanted to walk over there and snatch that parent the same way. If you could have seen the embarrassment on that face, my heart was torn in two.
I know that some days the load is unbearable. Take some time to cool off before you enter your family's atmosphere. Don't leak your hurt on them. They had nothing to do with it. Hurting people hurt people. Give your grief, pain and frustration to God. Walk in with a smile. Remember they haven't seen you all day. Don't let the first thing they see be a mad face or an angry look. Open the door and shout,

"DADDY'S HOME!"** Then open your arms and get ready for your daily dose of love, hugs and welcome, as your children run to meet you.

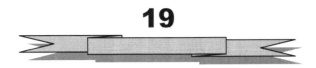

19

USE FAILURE

YOU DON'T DROWN BY FALLING IN THE WATER; YOU DROWN BY STAYING THERE.

THERE ARE NO SECRETS TO SUCCESS. IT IS THE RESULT OF PREPARATION, HARD WORK AND LEARNING FROM FAILURE. -- *COLIN POWELL*

All fathers must learn that we can teach more and do more with failure than with success. There is no teacher like pain and disappointment. Our children are going to experience seasons of failure and loss. Our reaction to their failures or mistakes will either drive the knife of grief and hurt deeper or begin to activate their healing.

When your children set out to do something and they have tried their best, let them know that it's okay to mess up. Life is made of ups and downs. Remember your reaction can be deadly.

Crisis is the birthing stool to a greater destiny.

- *Failure helps prevent making the same mistake twice.*
- *Failure can create climates of change.*
- *Failure can expose what is not working.*

- *Failure produces the power to search harder and reach higher to win.*
- *Failure can produce the ability to move to another place.*

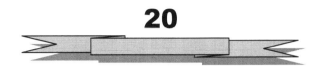

20

WALK IN FAITHFULNESS

Faithfulness is a powerful connection to your children. Fathers must and should teach their children what it means to be faithful. Faithfulness teaches a strong sense of duty and responsibility to what you have committed to do.

Faithfulness proves love…
"Love and faithfulness meet together; righteousness and peace kiss each other." Psalms 85:10 NIV

Faithfulness will out last time…
"…make your faithfulness known through all generations." Psalms 89:1 NIV

Faithfulness will be remembered…
"He has remembered his love and his faithfulness to the house of Israel; all the ends of the earth have seen the salvation of our God." Psalms 98:3 NIV

- ***Faithfulness creates seasons of joy.***
- ***Faithfulness produces comfort to those you love.***
- ***Faithfulness produces truth.***
- ***Faithfulness provides access to God.***
- ***Faithfulness demoralizes fear in those who are connected to you.***

Favored fathers are faithful fathers. What children need, no matter what age they are, is to be able to say that their father is faithful to them. Take the time to discipline yourself to be faithful.

21

BE A FRIEND

I can see as my children get older that my relationship with them is changing. I am no longer just the man who provides or the one who disciplines. I am now entering into a completely new role as being a father; a role which I seem to be enjoying very much. I am now entering into friendship with my children.

Friendship is nice! I have a 14-year-old son who is very smart and athletic. We seem to be growing closer as I keep the door open in my life and let him hang around. We go to movies together and I am always at his games, whether it be football or wrestling. I sit among his peers, joking and cutting up with them.

This new place in my life is one that I really see God in. The other day I was sitting around with the wrestling team and my son. So many of them have no one watching them and taking an interest in their lives. While I was sitting there, one of the kids came over to me and asked if I was Jerry's dad. I said yes. He began talking to me and immediately I could sense that this boy needed a father and a friend. I began to encourage him that he was doing great; at that time, he hadn't won a match. The next match he fought all the way up to the last few seconds. Mind you, he was loosing by points. However, in the last seconds he pinned his opponent. All the people stood including the team. Afterwards he came to me and thanked me for being there. This access to my son's life came to me not only by being a dad, but also by hanging out like one of the guys.

22

CONQUER INSECURITIES

Fathers decide what children remember; Mothers decide what they believe.

One of the greatest crises in our society today dealing with children is insecurity. A child who is raised with an absentee dad usually grows up with a big, black hole in their soul. Oh, they may succeed. They may even appear to be all together, but I can assure you that deep down in their heart they feel insecure.

- *Fathers build security.*
- *Fathers teach confidence.*
- *Fathers produce stability.*

All of these ingredients build a strong sense of love and security. Insecure means to be void of confidence, to be filled with anxiety, to be apprehensive.

When a child feels insecure, they will gravitate to anyone or anything that will make them feel secure. This is what I believe has happened to so many of our teenagers. They are having sex and getting pregnant because someone told them they loved them. They have such a poor concept of what real love is. They assume that love is just what someone says and not what someone has to show. **Where**

did they learn this? From absentee fathers who would not take the time to build them an identity. Spend some time with your children.

23

HEAL THE IDENTITY CRISIS

Fathers produce an identity. There is a phrase that applies to this key, "**Identity crisis.**" We are in a crisis of children not knowing who they are.

- 70% of juveniles in state-operated institutions come from fatherless homes. (Source: U.S. Dept. of Justice, Special Report, Sept 1988)
- 85% of all youths sitting in prisons grew up in a fatherless home.

Can you see the devastation to children who are not being raised with their fathers in the homes?

Maybe you are a father whose children are all grown. Let me encourage you to go ahead and make the changes right now. Repent to the Lord, speak to your children and let them know that you realize you should have been there more. Let them know that you want a relationship with them. Go ahead and take control; identify them. If you are a father reading this who was raised without your father being there for you, go ahead and forgive him. Let go of all bitterness and do things differently than he did.

Be a father who wants to identify your children. This identity crisis knows no race barrier. It's not a racial problem; it's a society problem. Let's win this war. If you are a dad that is always there, then do what I'm going to do; start praying for those who aren't.

24

NURTURE INDIVIDUALISM

THE FOUR CORNERSTONES OF CHARACTER ON WHICH
THE STRUCTURE OF THIS NATION WAS BUILT ARE:
INITIATIVE, IMAGINATION, INDIVIDUALITY AND
INDEPENDENCE."
EDWARD VERNON RICKENBACKER

Let me first state that I am not advocating that a father should completely relinquish his right as the head. There are areas in our children's lives that have to be watched and monitored for healthy growth to take place; things such as monitoring what they listen to and what they watch…what they do in private for a long period of time. I have a problem when my children lock their doors in my house; my question is what are you doing that I haven't already seen? What is so private you have to lock your door?

However, we must give our children the liberty to develop some individual freedoms. As a parent, choose your battles carefully; let them win some. My concern is not so much winning all the battles, but to come out winning the war of raising them. What I am trying to say is GIVE A LITTLE! Let them feel that they are somebody.

- *Individualism produces confidence in the ability to communicate.*
- *Individualism provides a sense of freedom.*
- *Individualism creates the passion to develop your own identity.*

25

LIVE BY INTEGRITY

"IT'S NOT WHAT WE EAT BUT WHAT WE DIGEST THAT MAKES US STRONG; NOT WHAT WE GAIN BUT WHAT WE SAVE THAT MAKES US RICH; NOT WHAT WE READ BUT WHAT WE REMEMBER THAT MAKES US LEARNED; AND NOT WHAT WE PROFESS BUT WHAT WE PRACTICE THAT GIVES US INTEGRITY." FRANCIS BACON, SR. QUOTES

Integrity is very important. I believe that you teach integrity by living out the example in front of your family.

Integrity is the quality or state of being complete; unbroken condition; wholeness; entirety; the state of being unimpaired; perfect condition; soundness, **the quality or state of being of moral principle; uprightness, honest and sincere.**

The greatest teachers of integrity are dads. When we decide to be the example instead of just preaching what is right, our influence in our children's psyche deepens. When they watch you take back your neighbor's stuff, or give back the change that the cashier gave you that was too much, or adhere to what you have promised, you are building the necessary building blocks that produce wholeness in their minds. Those decisions will affect their entire life.

- *Integrity builds a greater legacy.*
- *Integrity can mend the brokenness around us.*
- *Integrity promotes trust.*

26

CONFRONT JEALOUSY

"For jealousy is the rage of a man: therefore he will not spare in the day of vengeance. He will not regard any ransom; neither will he rest content, though thou givest many gifts." Proverbs 6:34-35 KJV

Jealousy is a serious problem. It may appear cute when children are little, but it will destroy them when they get older. Godly fathers refrain from walking in jealousy and monitor those in the house that do.

Jealousy is a resentful suspicion of a rival or rivals. For instance, a husband could be jealous of another man or one child could be jealous of what the other has or is doing.

A father can stop jealousy faster than the mother can. His attention and willingness to sit down with his children calms the fear of not being noticed or recognized. What was it that caused Cane to kill Abel? Jealousy! We must control and stop the sin of jealousy among our children and with those they are in contact with.

- *Jealousy can poison a healthy relationship.*
- *Jealousy is the work of the flesh.*
- *Jealousy causes good people to fight.*

- *Jealousy creates an attitude of hate and resentfulness.*
- *Jealousy can destroy unity.*

DEMONSTRATE HONOR

"Honor your father and your mother, as the LORD your God has commanded you, so that you may live long and that it may go well with you in the land the LORD your God is giving you." Deuteronomy 5:16 NIV

VIRTUE IS THE FOUNT WHENCE HONOR SPRINGS.   BY CHRISTOPHER MARLOWE.

We must teach our children honor. Don't expect them to know how to show honor. Honor has to be taught and the earlier you teach it the deeper it will be embedded in their hearts.

We are not only to teach honor but also to exemplify honor in those we respect.

- ***Honor precedes favor.***
- ***Honor promotes favor.***
- ***Honor preserves favor.***

The proof of honor is giving. I was having a conversation with Bishop Don Meares about this very subject. His reply was powerful. "Is there any other way to show honor than by giving?"

He is right! I believe the true way to show honor is by giving! When we give gifts, we are showing honor! Let your children experience the power of giving from you first.

GRACIOUSNESS WILL PRODUCE FAVOR

"May God be gracious to us and bless us and make his face shine upon us." Psalms 67:1 NIV

For some time, men have walked away from this word. Graciousness doesn't sound very masculine does it? However, to be a favored father we must learn to show and speak to your children with the words of love, compassion and kindness.

We love to sound like a general speaking with commands and directness, using words that are laced with sounds of anger and tones that make us feel that we are in control. You will never be in more control than you are when you walk in graciousness.

Men can learn a lot from women. Women possess the ability to create a pleasant atmosphere around them. They labor to make sure they look good and smell great! What 1000 Philistines could not do to Samson, one woman did in a day. How? **Graciousness!**

- *Graciousness is showing kindness.*
- *Graciousness is being courteous.*

- *Graciousness is showing mercy.*
- *Graciousness is being charming.*
- *Graciousness is having compassion.*

29

SHOW LOVE

"If I speak in the tongues of men and of angels, but have not love, I am only a resounding gong or a clanging cymbal. If I give all I possess to the poor and surrender my body to the flames, but have not love, I gain nothing."1 Corinthians 13:1-3NIV

Speaking love is not enough. Just saying I love you really becomes weak when your actions say and show the opposite. What are we teaching our children when we say I love you and we are never around? What do you think goes through their young impressionable minds? What happens to their spirit when they look around and you are nowhere to be seen when they just had a great performance in front of their peers? A touch down or maybe a solo in the school choir…maybe they were being honored for something and when they looked, once again you weren't there.

What about what they hear and how you speak to your spouse? Are you showing love or just saying it?

- ***Love is the most powerful force in the world.*** (Love can hold up under all things.)
- ***Love provides peace.***
- ***Love is longsuffering***.

- ***Love believes the best... Love is a decision, not a feeling.***

Have you showed love today?

30

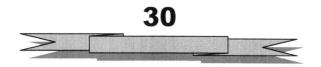

STOP, LOOK AND LISTEN

STOP, LOOK AND LISTEN! YOU MAY STOP A TRAIN WRECK!

STOP:
Stop what you are doing long enough to experience what is happening around you. Stop work. Stop watching television. A favored father is going to stop what is causing his family to feel neglected and start doing what it takes to build them and encourage them to succeed.

LOOK:
After you have stopped, take a look! Open your eyes. Notice what your family is doing. Do you know what your children are doing at school? Have you noticed whom they are hanging out with? I can tell a lot about someone just by meeting his or her friends. The course of your child's life could be depending on you taking a look. Do not ignore what you are seeing. They need you, man!

LISTEN:
Just stop what you are doing right now and open your ears. What do you hear? When you are around your family, open your ears and listen. Listen to what your children are trying to say.

A favored father can stop a massive train wreck in the relationship with his children if he will apply the stop, look and listen method to his life.

31

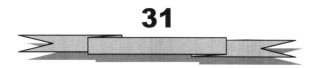

AVOID MANIPULATION

"LOVE COMES WHEN **MANIPULATION** STOPS; WHEN YOU THINK MORE ABOUT THE OTHER PERSON THAN ABOUT HIS OR HER REACTIONS TO YOU... WHEN YOU DARE TO REVEAL YOURSELF FULLY... WHEN YOU DARE TO BE VULNERABLE." DR. JOYCE BROTHERS

What many of us call love, God would call manipulation. It is so easy to only show love after we have received what we wanted from someone else.

Manipulation is something we learn early in life. A child starts to cry because it doesn't like being put down, or put to bed, or told no. Our reactions immediately teach that child that their persistency to cry, yell or pitch a fit causes us to give them what they want. **This is manipulation at its best**.

When we use the same approach with our children, it is wrong. A parent who only shows affection after the child did what they were told to do, is manipulating. We only give out compliments when we get what we want out of our children. This too is manipulation.

Let's avoid this false meaning of love. Love believes all things... love endures all things... love never fails.

Manipulation puts a strain on any relationship. (*I Corinthians 13*)

32

CREATE MEMORIES

Memories never die; they can only be replaced.
Fathers decide what children remember.
Mothers decide what they believe.

Our children are lacking strong memories of what they believe with the increase of absentee fathers in American homes. Most of the single parent homes are lead by women. These mothers are trying to do their best to build a structure of faith and hope in their children's life. The void of dads not in our homes is destroying the power of memory of what is valued and important.

Our memories are very important to experiencing peace and joy in our present life. Imagine memories of growing up or maybe you have those memories of an absentee dad. Can you imagine how painful it must be to live a life wondering why? Why wasn't my dad around more? Why didn't he spend time with me? Did he like me? Was I not good enough? Fathers, let's create great memories in our children's lives.

- *Pleasant memories create an attitude of joy and peace.*
- *Pleasant memories create comfort.*
- *A pleasant memory creates confidence to try.*

- *Memories are a replay of what was... imagination is a "pre-play" of what is about to be.*

33

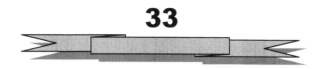

TEACH MANNERS

"LAWS ARE ALWAYS UNSTABLE UNLESS THEY ARE FOUNDED ON THE MANNERS OF A NATION; AND MANNERS ARE THE ONLY DURABLE AND RESISTING POWER IN A PEOPLE."
ALEXIS DE TOCQUEVILLE

Manners are what we use to be allowed to stay in other people's atmospheres. **Manners are necessary**! I was walking in the mall with my son and he was dragging his feet while he was walking beside me. I became agitated with the sound. I looked over at him and said, "PICK UP YOUR FEET, STAND UP, ACT LIKE YOU KNOW WHO YOU ARE." That afternoon while we were eating, once again I had to correct him. "Slow down, stop smacking…" He looked at me and said, "Why are you always watching me?" I replied with pride, "**Because you're my son!**"

That night the Holy Spirit began to mentor me. His words were that I teach manners because they are necessary for him to be accepted in someone else's atmosphere, not mine!

- *Manners teach etiquette.*
- *Manners teach protocol.*
- *Manners produce conduct.*

- ***Manners change behavior.***

Manners are the posture one assumes and has, when they are growing up and need to be taught. Fathers are the best instructors.

34

ALLOW QUESTIONS

I was sitting in my office the other day, pondering in my spirit what my mentor, Dr. Mike Murdock, and I were talking about in my truck. What questions have I failed to ask that have cost me the door to my next season?

I realized that most children are encouraged at a young age not to ask questions, but to listen. Yet until a question is asked, the answer remains hidden. ***What you fail to ask could be robbing you from something you need to know!*** Sitting around you every day is the answer to what you need to enter into your next season. If you fail to ask the question, you will fail to extract what is necessary to succeed.

As a favored father, encourage your children to ask as many questions as they can think of. They are developing the skills of learning much better than just sitting in a classroom listening to a teacher teach! ***When you ask a question, your mind is more acceptable to the answer.***

What question have you failed to ask that might have cost you your increase today?

- ***Answered questions tear down boundaries.***
- ***Answered questions bridge relationships.***

- *Unanswered questions create walls.*
- *Answered questions open doors of information.*

The Bible says, you have not because you ask not! (James 4:2)

35

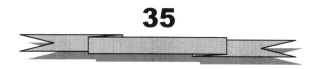

BE A MENTOR

Mentorship is success without the pain… Greatness without the wait… Victory without the loneliness…

A mentor is the greatest asset a father can become to his children. Be willing to take the time to mentor your children. The best time to mentor them is right at the end of loss or pain. I have found that my best fathering was not when my children were in trouble with me, but when they set out to accomplish something and in the process, they failed. At that moment, you are the voice that can steer them to being a winner.

Mentors are coaches. Cheerleaders really don't win games. Actually, most of them don't even know what's going on. But coaches are the ingredients that make bad players good and good players better! That is what a father really is; he is a coach and a gift given to a child by God!

I have a memory that I will never forget. This memory is why I played baseball as a child. One afternoon my father took me out and hit grounders, fly balls and pop-ups for hours. Every time I made a mistake or was afraid of the ball, he would come over to me, look me in the eyes and encourage me that being hit wouldn't hurt as bad as missing the ball. I remember looking into his eyes. His face was glistening with sweat. He had dark hair and this piercing look when he said to me, "Son, I love you… son, I'm your coach…listen to me and there's nothing you can't do or become…!" It was at that moment that I decided to play ball and to play hard to please my coach and my mentor, my father! The same is true with God!

36

TAKE VACATIONS

You want to really teach your children to honor the Sabbath? Take vacations at least once a year. The Sabbath has nothing to do with going to church. The Sabbath was to be a whole day and we don't go to church all day! The Sabbath was God's way of giving man one day to do something different. That is what the word means when God says keep the Sabbath holy... holy means different. There must be a day that we do something different. Even God needed a day to be different. On the seventh day, HE RESTED! God took a vacation, why can't we?

Someone once asked a Rabbi, how is it that the Jewish race has kept the Sabbath for so long? His reply, *"It's not the Jewish race that has kept the Sabbath, but it is the Sabbath that has kept the Jewish race."*

Your family will get to know you better when they can enjoy you outside the guidelines of the normal everyday routine of living. When they get to sit on the beach with you... or maybe ride a roller coaster with you... or just go out to eat. Take time off for them, not just for you!

37

DEVELOP A PRAYER LIFE

"I want men everywhere to lift up holy hands in prayer, without anger or disputing." 1 Timothy 2:8 NIV

One of the issues that have weakened our Godly culture is the lack of men who pray. Women seem to be better at this thing we call prayer then men do. Men have a hard time sitting for long periods of time, much less having to talk to the air and feel like we are not doing anything.

DON'T LET YOUR PRAISE REPLACE YOUR PRAYER...

Unfortunately, we have more people who desire to come to church to just sing or be entertained by dramas. Yet few seem to want to be there for the right reasons. I once heard someone say that if you bring in a singing group, the church will be full, but if you call a prayer meeting, you can't fill the first four pews. That seems to be the norm!

Men, we have to become men of prayer. Start somewhere, take 15 minutes a day and pray. Your family needs to see you pray!

- *Prayer changes things.*
- *Prayer produces peace.*

- ***Prayer creates a pleasant atmosphere.***
- ***Prayer is communication with God.***

Prayer is essential. Prayer is vital for a healthy walk with God.

38

BE A WORSHIPPER

"Therefore, since we are receiving a kingdom that cannot be shaken, let us be thankful, and so worship God acceptably with reverence and awe, for our God is a consuming fire." Hebrews 12:28-29 NIV

Worship like a woman, fight like a man! We need to learn how to worship. Worship is the most intimate part of our relationship with God. Intimacy is one word that men really have a hard time understanding. What does it mean to be intimate?

Intimacy means formula; it means closeness. For someone to be intimate, they are going to have to first be vulnerable and open to letting someone else in their private space. Men have a hard time being open and vulnerable. Somewhere we have been conditioned to think that being open or intimate is somehow betraying our manhood. I assure you this is as far from the truth as you can get. Men who are confident... men who have a secure identity... men who are sure of themselves have no problem with being intimate.

God expects us to worship him. The Bible says, "Let everything that has breath, praise the Lord..." Everyone who wants to praise God is allowed to, but there is no indication that everyone is allowed the access to worship Him. Worship has requirements. Why? Worship is intimacy with God. Worship is the place where God reveals His secrets. Worship is the place where the seeds of God are transferred. So men, let's start worshipping!

39

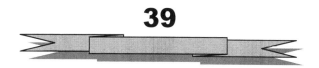

PURSUE SONSHIP

*"For you did not receive a spirit that makes you a slave again to fear, but you received the Spirit of **sonship**. And by him we cry, "Abba, Father." Romans 8:15 NIV*

*"You are all **sons** of God through faith in Christ Jesus..." Galatians 3:26-27 NIV*

*"...He predestined us to be adopted as **his sons** through Jesus Christ..." Ephesians 1:5 NIV*

Fathers formulate... Sons demonstrate... Grandsons authenticate.

To be a good father you must learn how to be a good son. If you are grown and you were not a good natural son, you must become a good spiritual son. God is our father; He has formulated and created what Jesus demonstrated so we, the spiritual grandsons, can authenticate what Jesus demonstrated. **We are the sons of God.**

Paul said we have ten thousand teachers but not many fathers. Teachers create an atmosphere of students... fathers create an atmosphere of sons (no gender). Students create an atmosphere of questions; however, sons create an atmosphere of inheritance. There's a big difference. This does not weaken the need for teaching, but addresses the greater need for fathers and sons.

Favored fathers are good sons.

40

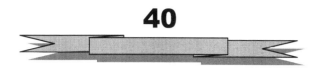

SOW SEED

The most powerful law of the universe is the law of sowing and reaping. Luke 6:38 says, *"Give and it will be given back to you, good measure, pressed down and shaken together; would men give back to you."* Either we are going to believe the Bible or we're not! If we can't believe Luke 6:38, then how do you know that John 3:16 is true?

They say that women do eighty percent of all the giving in our churches. Women seem to be the only reason church has survived as long as it has. The very nature of God is to give.

Satan steals… Man hoards… God gives!

- *Giving is the proof you've conquered greed.*
- *Sowing is the only way to guarantee your future.*
- *The seed that leaves your hand never leaves your life.*
- *Seed will always produce a harvest.*
- *If what is in your hand cannot pay for your vision, it is not your harvest; it's your seed.*
- *Seed sowing will demoralize the enemy in your life.*
- *Seed is the most dangerous word in the Bible.*
- *Favor is a seed before it can be a harvest.*

"As long as the earth remains, seedtime and harvest time will not cease..." Genesis 8:22

CONCLUSION:

Men, it's time to stand up and become a vital part in our homes and churches. The women have led the battle long enough. It's time for us to take our place…

STAND! FIGHT! WIN!

God has given us everything we need from helmet to silo to conquer and win this war. God is raising up men all over this country who are ready to enter the battle once again and fight for the right to worship…to give…to serve God with all of our hearts.

Our children are waiting for us to show up and be counted. I know that you are one of those men. I can sense that you are now taking your place in the ranks of spiritual warfare. Get ready for supernatural, double favor to explode in your life.

I consider it an honor and a privilege to be able to offer you this book. Take the time to look over my product list. I believe the difference between where you are and where you need to be is simple information.

Go to my website at **www.fogzone.net** I have put together devotionals and you can watch online services from the Favor Center Church. We have taken the time to accumulate the information you need to succeed because you matter!

"THERE'S NO LIFE LIKE A FAVORED LIFE!"

Dr. Jerry A. Grillo, Jr.

May I Invite You To Make Jesus Christ The Lord Of Your Life?

The Bible says, *"That if you will confess with your mouth the Lord Jesus, and will believe in your heart that God raised Him from the dead, you will be saved. For with the heart man believes unto righteousness; and with the mouth confession is made for salvation."* Romans 10: 9 &10

Pray this prayer with me today:
"Dear Jesus, I believe that you died for me and rose again on the third day. I confess to you that I am a sinner. I need your love and forgiveness. Come into my life, forgive me of my sins and give me eternal life. I confess you now as my Lord and Savior. Thank you for my salvation! I walk in your peace and joy from this day forward. Amen!"

Signed_____

Date _____

Yes, Dr. Jerry! I made a decision to accept Jesus Christ as my personal Savior today and I would like to be placed on your mailing list.

Name_____

Address_____

City, State, Zip _____

Phone_____Email _____

FAVORED PARTNERSHIP PLAN

Dear Favored Partner, God has brought us together... When we get involved with God's plans, He will get involved with our plans. To accomplish any vision it takes partnership...It takes people like you and me coming together to accomplish the plan of God.

WILL YOU BECOME ONE OF MY FAVORED PARTNERS TO HELP CARRY THE BLESSINGS OF GOD ACROSS THIS NATION?

In doing so, I believe there are three major harvests that you are going to experience...
   1. *Harvest of Supernatural Favor*
   2. *Harvest for Financial Increase*
   3. *Harvest for Family Restoration*

Sit down and write the first check by faith; if God doesn't increase you in the next months you are not obligated to sow the rest. Yes, Dr. Grillo, "I want to be one of your monthly partners...I am coming into agreement with you right now for my Three Miracle Harvests..."

Thank you,
Dr. Jerry A. Grillo, Jr.

PARTNERSHIP PLAN:

____**300 Favored Champion Partner:** Yes, Dr. Grillo, I want to be one of your Favored Champion Partners of **$42.00 a month**; involving my seed as one of the 300 who helped Gideon conquer the enemy of lack.

____**70 Favored Elders:** Yes, Dr. Grillo, I want to be one of you 70 Favored Elders of **$100.00 a month**. I want to be one of those who will help lift your arms so we can win over the enemy of fear and failure.

____**MY Best Seed:** $_____.____ Remember, no seed is too small and all seeds multiply. Seeds of nothing will produce harvests of nothing. Send your best seed today.

Name_____

Address_____

City _____State_____ Zip_____

Phone _____Email _____

Write Your Most Pressing NEED Below!

***Cut Out and Mail with Check or Money Order To
Dr. Jerry Grillo
P.O. Box 3707
Hickory, NC. 28603
If you desire to use your credit or debit card, go to
our website www.fogzone.net and use the donation
buttons.***

WATCH DR. GRILLO LIVE ON THE INTERNET.

Invite Dr. Grillo to Speak and Teach at Your Conference, Church or Leadership Meeting

To Schedule Him for Television or Radio Interviews,

Write To:
Fogzone Ministries
P.O. Box 3707
Hickory, NC. 28603

Or Email:
Fzm@charter.net

Fax Invitation To:
828-325-4877

Or Call:
1-888-Favor-Me (328-6763)

www.fogzone.net

STAY**CONNECTED,**
BE**BLESSED.**

From thoughtful articles to powerful newsletters, videos and more, www.fogzone.net is full of inspirations that will give you encouragement and confidence in your daily life.

AVAILABLE ON WWW.FOGZONE.NET
to Join the FAVORNATION and recieve a weekly update
text the word "FAVORNATION" to 22828

Design Your LIFE

Weekly Conference Calls from Dr. Grillo will help you grow in your relationship with the Lord and equip you to be everything God intends you to be.

Thursdays @ 9:00pm EST

Call: (712) 432-0075   Playback: (712) 432-1085
access CODE 118607#   access CODE 118607#

Dr. Jerry Grillo
STREAMING

Miss your local church service? Watch Dr. Gillo online, and see him LIVE
Sundays @ 10:30am EST & Wednesday @ 7:00pm EST

Dr. Jerry Grillo
VIDEO ARCHIVE

The Video Archive is a great way to watch Dr. Grillo where you want and when you want.

CONNECT WITH US

Join the FAVORNATION on your favorite social network

PUT DR. GRILLO IN YOUR POCKET

Get the inspiration and encouragement of Dr. Jerry Grillo on your iPhone, iPad or Android device! Our website will stream on each platform.

Thanks for helping us make a difference in the lives of millions around the world.

WWW.FOGZONE.NET

Made in the USA
San Bernardino, CA
27 January 2015